695

IF YOU LIVED IN BIBLE TIMES

Nancy S. Williamson

VICTOR BOOKS

a division of SP Publications, Inc.
WHEATON. ILLINOIS 60187

Offices also in Fullerton, California • Whitby, Ontario, Canada • Amersham-on-the-Hill, Bucks, England

Recommended Dewey Decimal Classification: 220.9

Suggested subject heading: Bible—History of Biblical Events.

Library of Congress Catalog Card Number:
ISBN: 0-88207-468-7

VICTOR BOOKS
A division of SP Publications, Inc.
P.O. Box 1825 ● Wheaton, Illinois 60187

Contents

IF YOU LIVED IN BIBLE TIMES

When Were Bible Times?

Bible times were a very long time ago. They were more than 2,000 years ago. Bible times began when God created our world. They continued about a century after the birth of Jesus.

This book does not tell everything about those years. Instead, it selects some of the interesting things to help you imagine what it would have been like to live in Bible times.

The time-line shows when some of the events of Bible times happened. It also shows when some important events of modern times took place. You can use it to travel back through history to find just when Bible times were.

CREATION

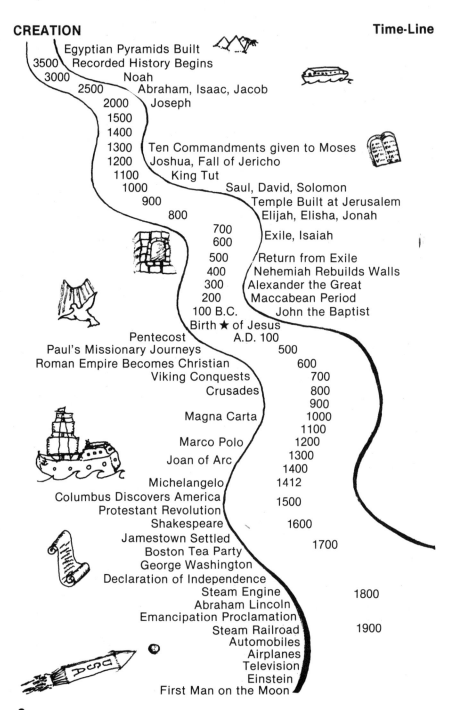

Egyptian Pyramids Built
3500 Recorded History Begins
3000 Noah
2500 Abraham, Isaac, Jacob
2000 Joseph
1500
1400
1300 Ten Commandments given to Moses
1200 Joshua, Fall of Jericho
1100 King Tut
1000 Saul, David, Solomon
900 Temple Built at Jerusalem
800 Elijah, Elisha, Jonah
700
600 Exile, Isaiah
500 Return from Exile
400 Nehemiah Rebuilds Walls
300 Alexander the Great
200 Maccabean Period
100 B.C. John the Baptist
Birth ★ of Jesus
Pentecost A.D. 100
Paul's Missionary Journeys 500
Roman Empire Becomes Christian 600
Viking Conquests 700
Crusades 800
900
Magna Carta 1000
1100
Marco Polo 1200
Joan of Arc 1300
1400
Michelangelo 1412
Columbus Discovers America 1500
Protestant Revolution
Shakespeare 1600
Jamestown Settled 1700
Boston Tea Party
George Washington
Declaration of Independence
Steam Engine 1800
Abraham Lincoln
Emancipation Proclamation
Steam Railroad 1900
Automobiles
Airplanes
Television
Einstein
First Man on the Moon

8

Where Were Bible Lands?

Bible lands were the areas around Palestine. Palestine is a hilly country. It is about the size of Israel today. It is 150 miles long and 50 miles wide.

The west border of Palestine is the Mediterranean Sea. A long row of hills runs along the coastline. In the south is Judea. The hills are very dry. The hot dry land goes south to the Red Sea and the Sinai Peninsula.

Farther north is Samaria. The land is more fertile. Grapes are grown on terraced hills. East of the hills is the Jordan River. It begins north at Mount Hermon and flows south through the Sea of Galilee. It ends at the Dead Sea. Beyond the river the hills are flatter. Finally they go into the Arabian Desert.

Mount Hermon is over 9,000 feet high. The Dead Sea is the lowest point on earth. It is 1,286 feet below sea level. The Dead Sea has no water outlet. The water evaporates. Salt and mineral formations are left around the Sea. Nothing grows or lives in the Dead Sea.

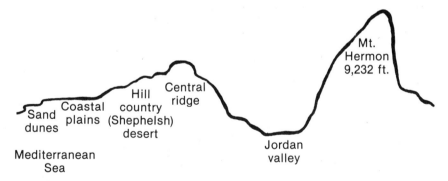

Topography of Palestine

Because Palestine is near the equator, the weather is mostly hot and dry. In winter snow is on the higher mountain tops. Most of the rain falls in the winter.

Every hill and valley, town and village, well and stream has its ancient story. You can read about these stories in your Bible.

Dry Hills of Judea

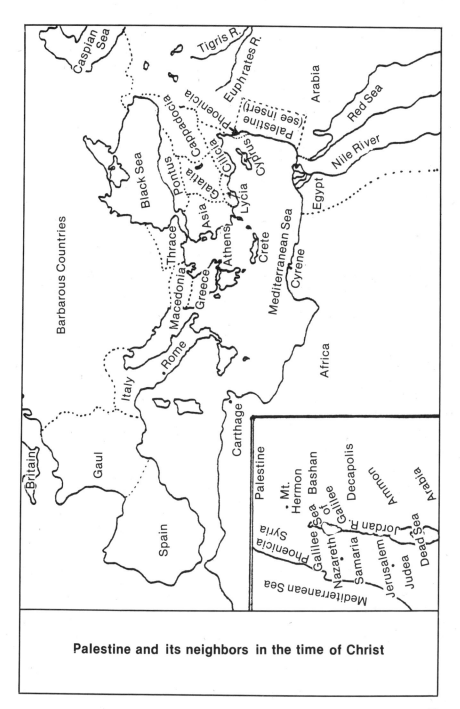

Palestine and its neighbors in the time of Christ

The map shows Palestine during the life of Jesus. It also shows the countries around Palestine.

Many of the villages in Palestine had high stone walls. The walls kept the enemies out. The walls had many gates in them. Traffic from the main highways entered the city through them.

The gates were closed at sunset. They opened again at sunrise. Sometimes in a large gate was a small door. This was just big enough for you to crawl through after the large gate had been closed for the night. This door was called the "eye of the needle."

**City Walls, Gate
and "eye of the needle"**

What Would Your Home Be Like?

Houses would be made of mud bricks. Windows covered with lattice-work were high above the street to keep out thieves.

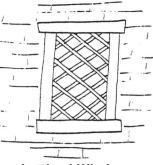

Latticed Window

After every rain the mud or clay roof had to be rolled with a small stone roller. A roller was kept on the roof. Holes had to be filled in with clay or mud. Leaks needed to be repaired at once or the whole roof might fall in during a rain. Sometimes drips coming down through the roof forced people to move their beds in the middle of the night.

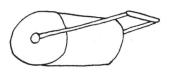

Stone Roof Roller

Because the wind often blew seed to the rooftop, grass grew there. It made a nice place for pet lambs to graze.

**The Outside of a
Palestinian House**

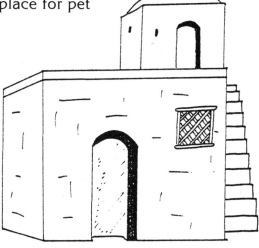

On the outside of houses people built stone stairways to the roof. Families used these stairways to get to the roof-top. There they could get away from the dust and noise of the streets. In the cool evening, Father told stories to the family. They would sit around his feet. Often a room was built on the roof for guests.

Houses had one large room. The room had two parts. There was a lower front part for animals. There was a higher back part for the family. A second room might be added to use as a shop for the head of the household. There he would carry on his trade as a carpenter, potter, weaver, or metal worker. A house was not a showroom for visitors. It was a home and workshop for the family. Usefulness and not beauty was important.

Straw was spread over the floor of the front part of the house. When it was cold chickens, goats, cows, and sheep stayed indoors. Pet lambs even slept with the children like puppies do today.

Inside a Palestinian House

A sort of fireplace was in the middle part of the room. When the fire burned down, a table was placed over it and covered with a carpet. The family could then sit on it to keep warm. Smoke from the fireplace went out through the latticed windows since houses had no chimneys.

The upper part of the room was for the family. The floor in this room was packed firm and smooth. Sometimes lime was mixed into mud and spread over the floor to harden. This floor could be swept and stayed dust free. In the floor was a covered hole for storing grain. The millstone for grinding was kept in one corner. Another hole in the floor was used to build a fire for cooking indoors.

There was little furniture. For example, tables were animal skin, leather, or linen spread on the floor. Beds were mats or blankets. They were rolled up and stored in small openings in the walls during the day.

Since the house was made of mud, the inside walls often had bulges. These bulges were hollowed out and filled with oil to float wicks for lamps. Another kind of lamp was an olive oil lamp made of clay. Palestinians feared the dark. Night was the time of danger from robbers and unfriendly neighbors. The oil lamp burned all night even in the poorest of homes. Cleaning the lamp and refilling it was a daily chore. A horn was used to fill the lamps.

Clay Oil Lamps

Doors were left open all day to show that visitors were welcome. A closed door showed that the family had done something which they were ashamed of. At sunset the door was closed. Father was the doorkeeper. He stayed near the door. He would answer the

Oil Horn

door and let visitors come in. At night he slept close to the door.

Ancient door locks were made of wood. The huge keys that turned the locks were also made of wood.

Ancient Key

A small box on the doorpost of a house showed that the owner was a good Jew. It contained pieces of parchment. Special verses from Scripture were printed on them. They were like the little leather boxes (phylacteries) that men wore.

Every village home had its kitchen garden next to the house. Here were most of the herbs and vegetables found in our own gardens.

What Would Your Family Be Like?

The Hebrew family liked to stay together. Children grew up, married, and had their own families. They built houses attached to that of the boy's parents. They could walk from rooftop to rooftop to visit.

A large family was a sign of God's blessing. Jewish people believed that "Children are a gift from the Lord" (Ps. 127:3).

Names were important to Jewish families. Often parents gave their children names which told something about the child, his parents, or their feelings about God. For instance:

Ezekiel means *God gives strength.*
Gamaliel means *reward of God.*
Isaac means *laughter.*
Matthew means *gift of God.*
Noah means *comfort.*
Solomon means *peaceable.*
Esau means *hairy.*
David means *beloved.*
Deborah means *busy as a bee.*

Eight days after the birth of a baby boy, he was taken to a priest for a service of dedication to God. He was given his name at this time.

Mother wanted her babies to have firm, healthy skin. Each day she rubbed the baby's skin with salt. Afterward she bundled him in white cloth. Bandage strips were wrapped around the outside to hold it in place. This held his arms and legs quite still. Mother be-

Baby Asleep

lieved this helped make them strong. These clothes were unwrapped several times a day. Then the baby was rubbed with olive oil and powdered myrtle leaves. Imagine how good it must have felt to be unwrapped and to be able to squirm around a bit?

Baby in Swaddling Clothes

How Would You Dress?

Children during the time of Adam and Eve, wore animal skin for clothing. After many years people learned how to make cloth from sheep wool, goat and camel hair.

After shearing, the wool or hair was beaten to get out the dirt and leaves. The mother and her daughters combed the wool. Then they spun it into thread. This thread was then woven into cloth on the family loom. Sometimes the cloth was dyed in a vat.

Ancient Loom

Different colors of dye came from plants and animals. The famous purple dye sold by Lydia (Acts 16:14) came from the murex shellfish of the Mediterranean Sea. It was valuable because only one drop was found in each fish. Because of its value, purple became the "royal" color for kings and noblemen.

After a while other kinds of cloth were made. Linen for the priests' clothes was made from flax. King Solomon imported linen yarn from Egypt at a very high price (2 Chron. 1:16). And silk, a luxury fabric, came from China. Cotton came into use about the end of the Old Testament time.

Only the wealthy had many clothes. Clothes were passed down in a family. Torn clothes were mended and patched.

When someone wanted to give a valuable gift, he would give a piece of clothing. Fashions did not change. Clothing was valuable for as long as it lasted. In fact, clothing was counted as wealth. It could be given as security for a debt. But the outer clothes could not be kept from its owner overnight because it was also used as a blanket.

Often the same clothing was worn both day and night. Pajamas were not worn during Bible times. Most people

Turban

Tunic

Outer Garment

Girdle

Sandals

Traditional Dress

had only one change of clothing.

Clothes were simple. They could be used in different ways. Most of the clothes worn in Bible times were loose-fitting. Usually they did not have sleeves, buttons, collars, or cuffs. A scarf around the head and shoulders was often

Scarf

worn.

A tunic was worn next to the body. It was something like a nightshirt. Wearing only a tunic was the same as being naked.

Over the tunic outer clothing was worn. This was large

The "Lap"

and loose. It could be used to wrap and carry things over the shoulder. These were called salmah or simlah. A fold in the salmah near the chest made a pocket called a lap. People carried money and other things in their lap. Even a little lamb could be carried in a lap. People never spent all the money in their lap. It was believed that the lap would then stay empty for a long time. If someone became angry at another person, he would probably shake his lap at him and shout.

The girdle was one of the most useful items of clothing. It was also ornamental and fun to put on. A very long rectangle of fabric was folded to the width wanted around the waist. A person, tree branch, or hook held one end of the girdle. The person putting on the girdle held the other end to his waist. Then he turned around and around until he got to the first end of the fabric. It was tucked in to hold everything together.

Girding Your Loins

The girdle was most useful when working or running. A person just pulled up the long skirts of his clothes and tucked them into the girdle. This gave more freedom of movement. When clothing was tucked in this way it was called girding up your loins.

According to Mosaic law Jewish men were supposed to wear a tallith. This was a mantle or short coat with a tassel at each of its four corners. One thread of each tassel was to be deep blue. The tassels were a reminder of the law of God and duty to keep it.

A cloth veil or turban was worn by men to protect their head and neck from the hot sun and strong desert winds.

A Tallith

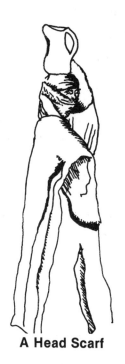

Women always wore a large head scarf. It covered the face like a veil. The scarf formed a cushion. The cushion was used to carry water pitchers from the well or other heavy loads on her head. Women's clothing was much like men's except it was brighter in color. It was also decorated with strings of coins or other ornaments. A woman could lift up the hem of her long dress to carry things.

Clothing was often embroidered with brightly colored threads. Wealthy people had their clothing embroidered with silks and gold.

A Head Scarf

Sandals stayed on the feet with a leather strap called a latchet. The soles were made of wood or leather. Sometimes they were made from the skin of a fish found in the Red Sea. People had to walk on dusty roads. They took their sandals off before going into a house or sacred place.

Men carried a staff used as a walking stick or cane. Sometimes it was beautifully carved or engraved. Some were decorated with gold or jewels.

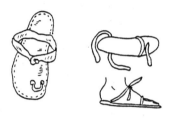

Sandals

Women wore earrings of gold or ivory. They wore necklaces of precious metal or pearls. Gold chains were sometimes worn on the ankles. Coins were also worn on chains around the neck or head. These were usually from the woman's dowry. They were kept by her as a kind of insurance. Then she would have some money if her husband suddenly divorced her.

Men wore signet rings. These rings had the owners' names on them and a special design. When the signet ring was stamped into wet clay or soft wax it left a design. The imprint was used as the owner's signature. Pharoah gave Joseph such a ring (Gen. 41:42).

Signet Rings

Men were very proud of their long beards. The beard was a sign of honor. Sometimes they trimmed their hair a little. Women often wore their hair in braids.

What Would You Eat?

The family did not sit down for breakfast together. Father carried a snack to work. Lunch was bread, olives, and fruit. Supper was usually vegetable stew and bread. On special occasions or when company was coming, meat was served.

When the sun was about to go down, mother began to get supper ready. Dishes were made of clay which had been hardened. There were no knives, forks, or spoons to eat with. Food had to be eaten with the fingers. Soft food couldn't be picked up. So pieces of bread were dipped in the soft food. This was called sop. Since silverware was not used, water was kept nearby to use at the end of the meal. Members of the family took turns holding a pitcher and basin. They poured water over one another's hands for washing.

The family always gave thanks to God before eating. One of the favorite blessings was "Blessed be Thou, O Lord our God, the King of the world, who produced bread out of the earth."

If the head of the family wanted to show a special favor to anyone, he chose the best pieces of meat or other food from the dish. Then he put them into the mouth of the guest with his own fingers.

Bread and milk were very important in the diet. Bible-time people liked spicy food. They cooked with salt, spices, garlic, saffron, and mint. Grapes were also important. The family used grapes for preserves, jellies, juice, pickles, and molasses. Other foods in Bible times were figs, dates, fresh and pickled pomegranates, almonds, pistachio nuts, citrus fruits, beans, lentils, wheat, peas, onions, melons, cheese, yogurt, and eggs poached in olive oil. The people also ate lamb, goat meat, beef, chickens, birds, and fish. There was no sugar.

Salt was used as a sign of friendship. Many times people who were going to harm another person would be tricked into eating salt with that person. Then he could not do the harm he had in mind. Harm could not be done to a friend.

When the family was going on a trip, mother always made cracknels or nikkuddim to eat along the way. They are thin, hard biscuits something like crackers.

Mother made the butter, but sometimes the children helped. Milk was put into bags or bottles made of goat skin. The family took turns shaking or beating it with sticks until the milk became thick and turned into butter. The bag could also be put on the ground and walked or jumped on to help the butter churn.

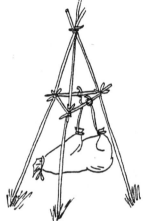

For an extra treat mother often mixed butter with honey. This was a delicious snack when spread on cracknels.

Fish was dried on the hot sandy beach. Then it was salted. It was turned over and salted again and again, until dried. It could then be

Skin Bottle for Churning Butter

kept for some time without spoiling. At times the dried fish were ground into fish flour. A traveler or shepherd carried the fish in a pouch to be eaten for lunch.

Good meat was hard to get in Palestine. When a farmer killed a cow, he lost his source of milk. He also lost power for his plow or threshing machine as well. If he killed a sheep or goat, he lost his source of wool and milk. The only way to preserve meat was to dry it in the hot sun, or pack it in salt or salt brine. Refrigeration and safe canning methods were not known.

Wheat and other grains were ground into flour. This was done on a grinding mill. The grinding mill had one large, flat round stone on the bottom. Another stone like it was placed on top. A hole was made in the center of the top stone. Grain was poured a little at a time through this hole. The top stone was turned around and around. The rubbing action of the two stones crushed and ground the grain into soft flour. The flour fell from the grinding mill onto a mat placed beneath it.

A Grinding Mill

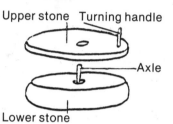

Upper stone   Turning handle

Axle

Lower stone

Yeast was added to dough to make it rise. The dough was made into flat, round loaves of bread. These were placed on the hot coals of a fire or on the outside of a hot clay oven to bake. They could be taken to a public oven to be baked. This oven was taken care of by a baker. He had to watch the fire all night so it wouldn't burn away (Hosea 7:6).

Cooking was done on a fire in a pit or on a fire in a clay oven. A fire heated the top of the round oven. A thin layer of batter was quickly poured over the surface of the oven. It stuck there until it was baked through. The thin layer of bread was easy to break into pieces to feed the family.

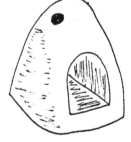

Clay Oven

Pots of different sizes were hammered out of sheet copper or brass. They were fitted with heavy metal handles so they could be hung over the fire. Clay pots were also used for cooking. Other cooking tools were ladles, dippers, bowls, and cups. They also used large storage jars for grain, wine, oil, and milk. There were even baby bottles and rattles made from clay.

Drinking water was always kept in a clay container near a window. It was kept cool by evaporation through the pores of the jug.

Ripe Wheat

What Kind of Money Would You Have?

A person's wealth was measured by the amount of goods he had, not by money. Abraham was a rich man with many sheep, cattle, silver, and gold. Job was the richest man in the country with thousands of animals.

In ancient times people did not keep gold and silver coins. They made bracelets and other jewelry out of their gold and silver. When they bought something, they paid for it with cattle or jewelry.

This sometimes caused problems. A person couldn't stuff animals or bracelets into a purse and carry them around. Also it was not easy to know just how much value to place on these items. So sometime later coins had to be made with each coin having a set value.

Long before the time of Jesus coins were used. In His day there was Roman, Greek, and Jewish money. The coin which is most often mentioned in the New Testament is the Roman denarius. This was worth about 15 cents. Jesus called the coin "that which is Caesar's," because it had an engraving of the head of the emperor. It was used for the payment of taxes. A denarius was considered a fair day's wage for a laborer.

Jewish coins did not have "graven images" of any person. This was because of the law against idolatry. The coins instead had pictures of such objects as a helmet or prow of a ship.

Denarius

The buying power of a coin changed from time to time, through good and bad times. In earliest times lumps of silver were used as money. The changing values of coins led to cheating. Money changers, publicans, and merchants became wealthy by being dishonest. They cheated people who knew little and were poor.

In Bible times the talent, or "round thing," seems to have been a metal ring weighing 3,000 shekels. This talent of silver was worth $2,000. Gold, in ancient as well as modern times, was worth about 15 times as much as silver. A shekel of gold was valued at about $10. A talent of gold was valued at about $30,000.

Shekel   Denarius

Farthing

Half Shekel   Daric

Ancient Coins

How Would You Tell Time and Measure Things?

People in Bible times were never in a rush. In fact, Bible lands were called "the unhurried East." If a job wasn't completed in one day, it would wait until another day, week, or year. If a father could not complete some work, perhaps his son would, or even his grandson.

The people still needed to tell time. There were no clocks or watches in Bible times. The sun was used instead. A person watched his shadow grow longer and longer. He measured the length of his shadow. Then he could tell about what time it was.

Some people in Bible times used a type of sundial called a shadow clock. The head of the clock was turned to the East at sunrise. A shadow fell on the long board. The board was marked into hours. At noon, the head was turned to the West. The shadows then fell on the afternoon hours. The sundial was used mostly by rich people.

A Man Using Shadow Clock

A water clock was used by people who lived near Palestine. People in Palestine probably used it too. It was something like an hour-glass. It worked by water flowing into a certain size cistern within a certain amount of time.

Today the clock lets us know when it is time to stop work and go home. In Bible times when a person was tired and wanted to go home from work, he'd say, "How long my shadow is in coming!"

The week had six workdays. The Sabbath day followed.

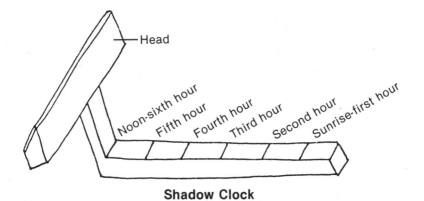

Shadow Clock

It was the day of rest. The holiness of the Sabbath was protected by Mosaic laws, such as:

No one could work on the Sabbath.

Extra food for the Sabbath was to be made the day before.

No fires could be started.

Only fifteen furlongs (one and a half miles) could be traveled on the Sabbath.

Today months are based on the movement of the sun. The moon was used to measure the changing of seasons in Bible times. The new moon was cheered by the blowing of the shofar as the beginning of a new month. There are only two seasons in Palestine—summer and winter. There are special seasonal periods. The barley harvest is during our springtime. The wheat harvest is during our early summer. The harvest of grapes is during our midsummer. The time of sowing is during our fall. Beginning in spring, the months run as follows: Nisan, Iyar, Sivan, Tammux, Ab, Elul, Tishri, Marcheshvan, Chisleu, Tebeth, Shebet, and Adar.

No specific way to measure area is mentioned in the Bible. Usually it was measured by the yoke—the amount of ground that a yoke or pair of oxen could plow in a day. This is about two-thirds of an acre.

Linear measure was based on parts of the human body.

Months and Seasons

Oct.	Nov.	Dec.	Jan.	Feb.	Mar.	Apr.	May	June	July	Aug.	Sept.	Oct.
Bul/March-esvan	Kislev/Chisleu	Tebeth	Shebat	Adar	Nisan/Abib	Iyar/Ziv	Sivan	Tammuz	Ab	Elul	Tishri/Ethanin	

- First Rains
- WET SEASON
- Snow on Mountains
- Late Rains (Sprinkles)
- DRY SEASON
- Intense Heat (Heavy Rains)
- Plowing and Sowing
- Olive Harvest
- Fig Harvest
- Flax Harvest
- Cereal and Barley Harvest
- Wheat Harvest
- Vine Tending
- Summer Fruit Harvest
- First Fig Harvest
- Grape Harvest
- Second Fig Harvest
- Dedication/Lights
- Purim
- Passover/Firstfruits
- Weeks/Pentecost
- New Year/Trumpets, Atonement, Booths

Months and Seasons

The smallest unit was the fingerbreadth (finger width), a little less than an inch. Four fingerbreadths made a handbreadth, or palm. Three palms made one span. A span was the distance between the tip of the thumb and the tip of the index finger of an outstretched hand. Two of these spans totaled a cubit. A cubit was the distance between the elbow and the tip of the longest finger. Many different cubits were used. Goliath had a height of six cubits and a span. He must have been nine feet six inches tall!

Larger distances were figured in the terms of a man's step or pace. A step was approximately 30 inches. "A little way" was over three miles. This distance could be walked easily in an hour. The "day's journey" was the distance which one could walk in about seven or eight hours. This was done during the daytime. A rest time was also included. The distance traveled in a day was about 20 miles.

Jugs that held liquids were stamped with a seal. The seal indicated the amount of weight they would hold. Round stones were also marked with their exact weight. They could be used with balance scales. They were used to help measure the weight of grains, vegetables, and other dry crops.

Merchants sometimes had two different sets of weights. One set of weights was used when they were buying. Another set was used when they were selling. They used these to cheat others. But this was against the laws of God. Deuteronomy 25:13 reads, "Do not cheat when you use weights and measures. Use true and honest weights and measures so that you may live a long time in the land."

The Hebrew shekel was the common weight. It was equal to about two-fifths of an ounce. Greek and Roman weights were used in Jesus' time. They were the libra or pound. They weighed about 12 ounces.

Balance Scale

Chart of Measurements

Length

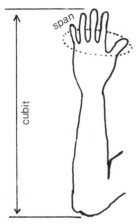

Cubit—measured from elbow to tip of middle finger = 17.5 inches.

Finger—width of a finger = ¾ inch.

Handbreadth—width of hand at base of fingers = 3¼ inches.

Span—from top of little finger to tip of thumb with hand stretched out = 9½ inches

- Six cubits = one reed
- Pace is equal to one step = 36 inches
- Mile = 1612 yards or 4836 feet
- Day's journey = 10 to 20 miles

Liquid Measure

Log = ⅔ pint
Hin = 3 quarts + ¾ pint
Bath = 5 gallons + 1 pint

Dry Measure

Kab = 1 quart
Omer = 2 quarts
Seah = 6 quarts + 1½ pints
Ephah = 3 pecks + 3 pints
Homer = 8 bushels
- A donkey load = 10 baths or 1 homer

Balance Scale and Stone Weights

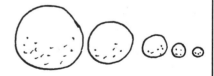

Where Would You Shop?

Businesses and trades in the larger cities grouped themselves on certain streets and in special marketplaces. There was the street of potters. There was the street of silversmiths. There was the street of carpenters.

To these marketplaces came sheep, calves, and goats of the shepherd, vegetables and fruits from the farms, fish from the Sea of Galilee and the Mediterranean. The traveling merchants came with their shiny brass utensils. The dyers came with their bright fabrics. The money-changers and tax collectors came. The beggars and pickpockets came to try their trades. Citizens came to buy, window shop, and meet new friends.

Here was a cross section of the life of the community. It was a scene of noise and bustle and excitement. Wide-eyed children found something exciting. Curious strangers found something new. The marketplace centered around the main gates to the city.

Marketplace

How Would You Travel?

Fully Loaded Donkey

Transportation was different than it is today. There were very few good roads in Bible times. The average road was not taken care of. They were dusty in the summer. They could not be used in the rainy season. When anyone important traveled along a road, a herald went ahead of him. He told the villagers to make the road straight. They did this by filling in the holes.

Bible times people could not take a trip by car, bus, train, or airplane. There were none. They walked everywhere. Sometimes the women and children would ride on donkeys.

Camels at Oasis

Donkeys were the most important way to travel. They carried people from one place to another. They carried heavy loads on their backs. Oxen were also used. They pulled carts with heavy loads.

Camels were used for travel to far away cities. Traders formed camel trains or caravans. By traveling in caravans the merchants could have companionship and protection. Along the caravan routes were stops at oases—water holes, or springs in the desert. The travelers then would stay in the inns which were built there.

Wagons were also used. The wheels were made of three or four heavy wooden planks. They were put together with two crosspieces and shaped into a circle. Then these were held together by a tire of iron or rawhide.

Camel

Ox Cart

Caravan

Ships were used for travel on the seas. They were powered by sails or by slaves who rowed them. The people who lived along the Jordan River and its lakes used small boats for fishing. The boats were also used for transportation. They were built of overlapping boards. Then they filled the spaces with fiber and pitch to make them watertight. The boats were very useful. Sometimes favorable winds made the use of sails possible. But most of the time the boatmen had to use their oars. Rafts were made of inflated animal skins covered by a wood platform.

Along the rocky shores were fine harbors. The people of Phoenicia were great shipbuilders. The merchant mariners of Phoenicia were the traders of the ancient world. In the last four centuries before Christ and during New Testament times, great fleets of ships carried goods. The goods came from Egypt, Syria, Phoenicia, and Greece. They were on route to the western Mediterranean as far as Rome, Sicily, and Spain. It was on one of these ships that Paul had a shipwreck (Acts 27).

Phoenician Merchant Ship

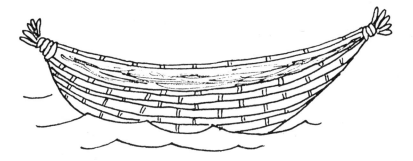

Woven Papyrus Boat

Skin Boat

Ancient Ships

Chariots were used mostly by the rich or soldiers in times of war. They were pulled by fast-running horses.

Chariot

Would You Go To School?

Education was important. Only boys went to school. They could go to school when they became 6 years old. The school was attached to the synagogue.

A boy never forgot his first day at school. At dawn he went with his father to the synagogue. There he heard how Moses received the Law. Next he went to his teacher's house and was welcomed. He was given a slate with Old Testament passages written on it. The slate had honey on it which he had to lick off. Next he ate small cakes with Bible verses written on them. As he ate the honey and cakes the child learned why he went to school. He was to learn and take in the teachings of the Old Testament, just like his body took in the honey and cakes.

The Jewish Bible (the Old Testament) was his only textbook. He learned by repetition. He also learned how to read and write the Hebrew language.

Pupils sat cross-legged on mats placed on the ground, or on low stone benches. The teacher sat in front on a high stool.

School

People spoke Aramaic in Palestine in Jesus' day. Children needed help in reading and understanding the ancient Hebrew Scriptures. Instruction was given orally. The children were not encouraged to think for themselves. They were only to remember the Law.

Schools for older pupils taught botany, geography, mathematics, grammar, and literature.

Would You
Have To Do Chores?

Flock of Sheep

Mothers did many of the same chores as today's home-
makers. They baked bread or cakes. They made delicious
stew. They swept the house and sewed. Mothers in Bible
times ground meal. They also drew water from the well.
They carried heavy jars filled with water. Their husbands
did much of the farm work. The husbands also threshed
grain, killed animals for meat, and brought in the
firewood.

Villages were built near wells or springs in order to have water for the people and animals. Women went to the well in the early morning or evening when the air was cool. Children often helped with this chore.

As children grew up they took on more responsibility in the home. Girls were taught spinning, weaving, sewing, grinding grain, and baking bread. They also had to care for younger brothers and sisters. They also helped with out-

Drawing Water at the Well

side chores. They learned to draw water from the well. They watched over the flocks. They filled the trough for their father's sheep.

Boys learned their father's trade as their future occupation. They helped their fathers with the flocks and herds. Some worked in the fields and vineyards. Joseph, Gideon, Saul, David, Elisha, and Jesus all worked for their fathers. It was a Jewish law that everyone should learn a trade to support himself. The great Apostle Paul was trained to be a tentmaker.

It was also the father's job to teach his son the Law and the meaning of the Jewish faith. It was the mother's job to teach manners.

How Would You Play?

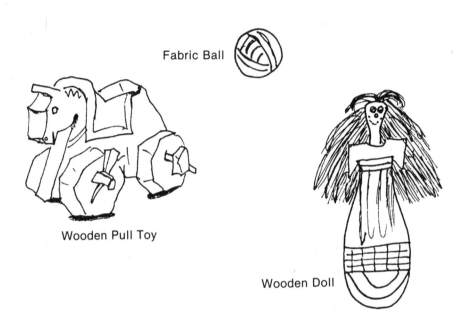

Fabric Ball

Wooden Pull Toy

Wooden Doll

Ancient Toys

Children were not always helping with chores or studying. They played with toys and games much like today. There were rattles and toy animals. There was miniature doll house furniture and puppets. Children had wooden pull toys, balls made from fabric, and marbles. They had whistles and dolls. They played hopscotch and leapfrog.

Sometimes a hole was dug in the ground. Children competed to see who could throw the most stones into the hole from several feet away. Other times they pretended to be a grownup and played house, wedding, or even funeral.

Both children and grownups used slingshots and bows and arrows for target games.

Would You Be Disciplined?

Then, as now, children found many ways to get into trouble. They were so likely to act foolishly that it was written, "Foolishness is bound in the heart of a child, but the rod of correction shall drive it far from him" (Prov. 22:15).

Hebrew parents knew the importance of correcting, chastening, and disciplining a child while he was young. This was to spare him more drastic punishment by civil authorities (police) later in life for wrong doing.

There are many references to "rods" in Proverbs and other biblical books. It seems that Hebrew parents often used spanking. Hebrew parents believed that they showed true love for their children when they brought them up strictly. "He who spares the rod hates his son, but he who loves him is careful to discipline him" (Prov. 13:24, NIV).

Would You Have A Pet?

Household pets seemed to be members of the family. Just like today, they were loved, fed, and protected. Pets made the home happy and full of life. They gave hours of fun for the children.

The most exotic pets in Bible times were the apes and peacocks. They were brought to Solomon from the East (1 Kings 10:22).

Dogs were family pets (Matt. 15:27). Lambs were a favorite pet. They were brought right into the home. Nathan affectionately described a pet lamb in his parable in 2 Samuel 12:3, "But the poor man had nothing, save one little ewe lamb, which he had bought and nourished up. And it grew up together with him and with his children. It did eat of his own meat, and drank of his own cup, and lay in his bosom, and was unto him as a daughter."

Palestinian Lamb

Would You Have To Obey Any Special Laws?

There were the laws of God which were given to Moses on Mount Sinai. These were the Ten Commandments. You can read about them in Exodus 20. The Books of Leviticus and Deuteronomy contain many other laws which Moses gave to the people of Israel.

One of the Mosaic laws said that a man must build a low wall around the roof of his house. This would protect those who were on the roof from falling off. This law, found in Deuteronomy 22:8, showed the people how much God loved them and wanted to keep them from getting hurt.

There were laws that were made up by the Pharisees and handed down from generation to generation. They were the "Tradition of the Elders."

One of these traditions said that bowls with brims had to be completely covered in water when washed. Without brims it was not necessary.

You could not kill a fly on the Sabbath day. That was considered hunting. Hunting was work. Tradition would not allow work on the Sabbath. A stick could not be pushed forward into the earth on the Sabbath, for that was plowing. But is was alright to drag the same stick behind your back. There was always debate as to whether or not you could eat an egg laid on the Sabbath. Children were not allowed to run or skip when playing on the Sabbath.

Some traditions were just good manners. To show respect, young men stood up in the presence of their elders. But one tradition said when a Hebrew man approached another on the road, he bowed to the ground to show respect.

What If You Were Sick?

The Bible mentions most of the illnesses we know today. There was alcoholism, blindness, lameness, neuroses, palsy, and problems of old age.

Today, science has found vaccines and medicines that have done away with some of the diseases of Bible times. For example, science has overcome the Bubonic plague. This is probably the disease that killed seventy thousand people (2 Sam. 24:15). Today's families accept the cure of disease without too much thought. People in Bible times always gave thanks to God for overcoming disease, whatever the means.

Luke was a physician. He did not have many surgical instruments to work with. Those he did have were very much like those in use today. Surgeons of Bible times tried operations of all kinds. However, without the knowledge of medicines to stop pain and heal, these were not very successful.

Most people used their own home remedies. They were made of roots, herbs, and berries. The recipes were passed down from generation to generation. External medication was used by most people. Wounds and bruises were cleaned with water or wine, covered with olive oil, and then bandaged. Oil was used for anointing and medicinal purposes. Soothing ointments and salves were made from various herbs.

Without the conveniences of modern plumbing like we have today, cleanliness was difficult. Most people used streams for bathing. Some would take a sponge bath in their home. After the bath, the body was rubbed with perfumed oil. Spikenard was the most costly of oils. Most people used the cheaper olive oil.

Would You Get Married?

When a boy became 13 years old and a girl became 12 years old, the family made plans for them to be married. The actual marriage did not take place for a few years. The couple was said to be engaged or betrothed.

The boy's family had to pay the girl's family for her loss to them when the marriage finally took place. It was expected that every boy would get married. There was no word for "bachelor" in the Hebrew language.

Part of the wedding ceremony was at the bride's house. In the evening the groom arrived. The groom took the veil from the bride's face and placed it on his shoulder while the family gave their blessings. The bride and groom went to their new home—usually the groom's. All the friends who had been invited to the wedding feast waited in the dark with lamps to light the couple's way.

Would You Have Music?

Music and dancing were important. There were three types of musical instruments—string, wind, and percussion. Harps, lyres, flutes, timbrels, drums, trumpets, and cymbals were the main instruments.

The stringed instrument, the kinnor, was similar to a guitar. It had gut strings and a stretched-skin sounding board. One of the most popular of the percussion instruments was the timbrel, or tambourine. It was a light wooden hoop with rawhide stretched tightly across its surface.

The cornet, or the trumpet, came from the curved horn of an animal. Later it was made of silver and had a bright sharp tone. Like our church bells it called people to worship. The cornet made from a ram's horn was called a shofar. It called people to war. It was also used to announce the beginning of each new month. Bible time dancing was rhythmic steps in circular movements. Music was the tapping of tambourines or other percussion instruments (Ex. 15:20).

Shofar

Double Flute

Worship in the Temple used music in the singing of Psalms. David even arranged a Temple choir and orchestra to "sing and to play joyful music." It is described in 1 Chronicles 15:16-24.

Bagpipes also were used during Bible times (Dan. 3:5).

Timbrel

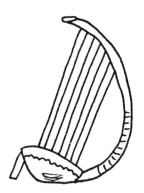

Harp

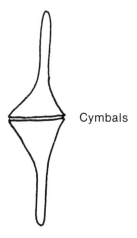

Cymbals

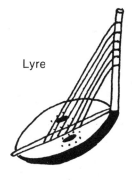

Lyre

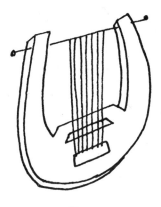

Harp

Ancient Musical Instruments

Would You Participate in Athletics?

The famous Olympiad began in 776 B.C. Only Greeks were allowed to enter these games. The games opened in a stadium where an orator (speaker) made a speech praising Greece and her athletes.

For five days there were athletic contests of every kind. They had boxing, wrestling, and foot races. The Pentathlon had five events—broad jump, discus throw, javelin throw, two-hundred yard dash, and wrestling match. Winners were crowned with a wreath. They were cheered and honored. They were immortalized in sculpture and song.

In a hippodrome (stadium) nearby horse races were held. The main event was a four-horse chariot race.

Besides Olympia, contests were held at religious festivals. Some of the contests were in dancing, speaking, singing, poetry, and playing the harp and flute.

What Occupation Would You Have?

There were many trades, occupations, and professions in Bible times.

Perhaps a person owned a vineyard. Grapes would be his main crop. He would be very busy looking after the vines during the summer months. Then in the fall it would be harvest time. Usually someone had to stay in the vineyard during the time the grapes were ripening. He had to see that thieves did not come in and steal the grapes. After the grapes were all picked from the vines, some were tramped on to get their juice. The grapes and juice were taken into the village to be sold at the marketplace.

Other farmers grew grains and vegetables. All of the work had to be done by hand. There were no machines like farmers use today. Oxen, donkeys, or horses helped pull the plow. The farmer had to watch carefully and not look backward to guide the animal to make straight rows. He also had to put all his weight on the plow to keep it in the ground.

Merchants and traders sold their crops and wares in the marketplace. They had to be very good at understanding weights and measures and how money was to be exchanged.

Potters were important. They made bowls, pitchers, lamps, and many other things for people to use every day.

Other men worked with metal, gold, silver, copper, and iron to make utensils, tools, and weapons.

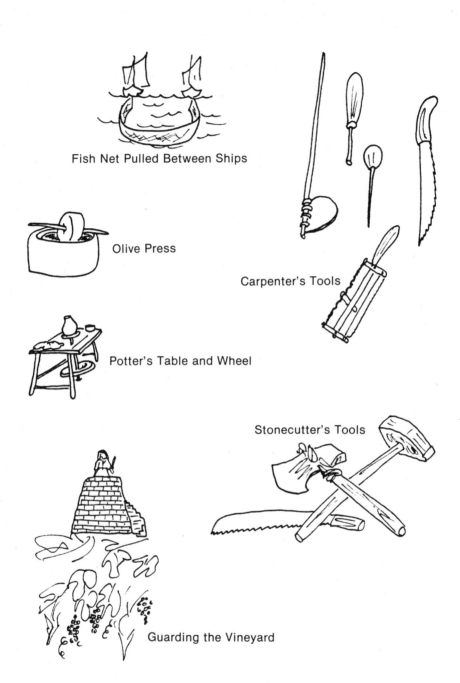

Fish Net Pulled Between Ships

Olive Press

Carpenter's Tools

Potter's Table and Wheel

Stonecutter's Tools

Guarding the Vineyard

Tools of Trades

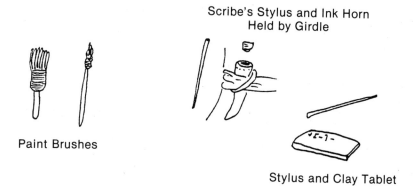

Scribe's Stylus and Ink Horn
Held by Girdle

Paint Brushes

Stylus and Clay Tablet

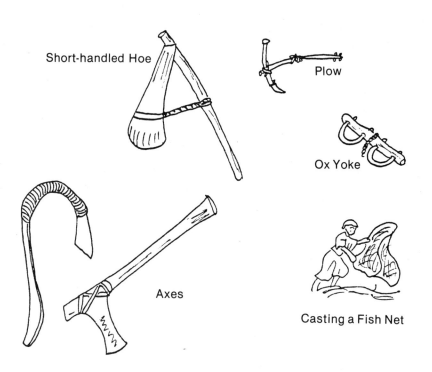

Short-handled Hoe

Plow

Ox Yoke

Axes

Casting a Fish Net

Tools of Trades

57

Some people worked at making clothes and others worked with leather. Some were fishermen, hunters, or secretaries (called scribes). There were even doctors and lawyers. Many people worked for the government. Some collected taxes.

People had to have houses to live in, buildings to work in, and places to worship in. There were people who were builders. Even women sometimes helped spread mud on the outside of the buildings.

People in the same trade generally lived on certain streets or in certain areas of the city. In this way they were in close contact with each other. At times they banded together to form pressure groups to protect their sources of income. This was probably an ancient type of worker's union.

If you lived in Bible times you could be a potter, carpenter, or fisherman. You could be a mason, metal worker, or tanner. You could be a dyer, tentmaker, merchant, or money changer. You could be a banker, day laborer, physician, weaver, or vinedresser. You could be a shepherd, basket maker, brickmaker, stonecutter, gem cutter, farmer, lawyer, or teacher. You could even be a mathematician, architect, astronomer, or musician.

How Would You Worship?

Public worship was conducted in the Temple or synagogues. The word for "meeting together" is *synago*. The synagogue was built in the most important location in the town. It was always higher than other buildings because it was built on a hill or had a tall spire on the top.

People went into the synagogue through two doors under an archway. The small door which led to a staircase and a gallery was used by the women and children. They could not take part in the services.

Worshipers faced the pulpit. Teachers and readers faced the worshipers from behind the pulpit. Behind the teachers was a large curtained alcove. A lamp was always burning in front of the alcove. This alcove contained the "Ark" where the precious Law books were stored.

Everyone went quietly into the synagogue. They were taught that no one must rush into the House of God. Also everyone had to be properly dressed.

Very religious men wore small leather boxes strapped to their foreheads and left arms. The boxes were called phylacteries. They contained pieces of parchment with Scriptures written on them. The Scriptures were Exodus 13:2-10; 13:11-17 and Deuteronomy 6:4-9; 11:13-22.

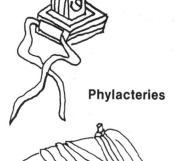

Phylacteries

An important part of the religious life was a pilgrimage to the Temple. The entire family could go if they wanted to. Men were required to make these pilgrimages. The Bible (Luke 2:41-42) tells of one such trip Jesus took when He was only 12 years old. This trip was to attend the Feast of Passover in Jerusalem.

Passover Feast began when God's chosen people, the Hebrews, were to be freed from slavery in Egypt. On the 10th day of the month Abid, the head of each family chose a perfect male lamb to be roasted. Blood from the slain lamb was sprinkled on the doorposts of their home. The blood indicated that the household belonged to God. Exodus 12:1-51 tells the story of the first Passover.

In later times this annual feast differed from the original. Passover was held from the 14th to the 21st of the month Nisan. This was a season of rejoicing. It was the beginning of the Jewish religious year. During the preparation for this feast the house was cleaned and all leaven (yeast) and leavened bread was removed. Leaven was a sign of fermentation and contamination. Unleavened bread was a sign of the hard times they had under Pharaoh.

The second great feast was Pentecost. It was also called the Feast of Harvest. This took place 50 days after the beginning of Passover. Pentecost lasted only one day. Offerings of bread made from the new wheat crop were made at the Temple. Until this feast was celebrated, the produce from the harvest could not be eaten. Pentecost was a dedication of the crops to God.

The Feast of Tabernacles or Booths was the most joyful and popular of all. When the family prepared for this feast a lot of work had to be done. It was held in the fall when the crops had been harvested. The family built a wood booth and covered it with branches. This booth was large enough for the entire family to be inside. This booth was to remind them of the time when the people of Israel lived in tents in the desert.

The feast of Booths included prayers, songs, dances, and a ceremony of water. Water was poured out and

Festival of Booths

Model of Temple

David's City and Temple Mount

prayers made for ample rain for the next year's crops. There was also a time of thanksgiving for the present year's harvest. Problems were not worried about at this time. It was a time of celebrating God's goodness.

The Feast of Purim honored the memory of the Jews being freed from massacre in Babylon. It was a time to remember the wisdom of Queen Esther and her uncle, Mordecai. Their story was always read during this feast (Es. 9:26-28).

The Feast of Lights celebrated the time that Judas Maccabaeus made the enemy leave the Temple. This event took place during the time of history between the Old and New Testaments. It is not recorded in our Bible. During this feast the Temple was bright with lights. People marched into the temple with palm leaves.

The first day of each lunar month was observed as a holy day. All work stopped and public worship was lead in the Temple. On the 13th day of the month watchmen stood on the hills around Jerusalem to see the sky. As soon as they saw the new moon they hurried to tell the rulers. Immediately the news was sent throughout all the land by torches from the tops of the hills. Trumpets were sounded, offerings were made, and great banquets were held (1 Sam. 20:5-29).

The Day of Atonement was a very special day for the Hebrews. It celebrated God's help and forgiveness of their sins. Moses commanded that this be a day of fasting. On this day, the High Priest was permitted to enter the Most Holy Place in the Temple. Then he sprinkled goat's blood on the mercy seat for the sins of the people of Israel. By the shedding of blood God forgave sins. Another goat was sent away into the wilderness to carry away the sins of the people.

Would you like to have lived during Bible times? Your life would have been quite different from today. So much—especially in the area of worship—changed after Jesus' life on earth. It's nice to live today—for more reasons than one!